Woodhall

on old picture p(

GW00673210

Brian and Shirley Prince

1. The Spa Baths and Pump Room on a postcard by Valentine of Dundee published about 1904. The Lord of Woodhall Manor, Thomas Hotchkin, found that salty water, rising from a shaft originally sunk in an attempt to discover coal, benefitted his gout. He created the original Bath and Pump House in 1838, though it was improved in 1887-8 by Bath's city architect. This summer scene includes a lady with parasol and boy in sailor suit.

Designed and Published by
Reflections of a Bygone Age
Keyworth, Nottingham
1992

ISBN 0 946245 56 8

£2.95

INTRODUCTION

Our collection of postcards of Woodhall Spa gives us great pleasure, and finding another card for it is an exciting experience. Our pleasure is shared by those who see the cards and it was for this reason that we decided to extend their viewing to a wider audience. We feel sure they will serve to recall happy memories for an older generation and give newer residents and visitors a picture of Woodhall Spa in days past.

Such cards enable you to see and appreciate, for instance, the magnificent buildings which once occupied Royal Square and the beautiful little church on the opposite corner, St Andrew's, of which only the churchyard remains today.

Picture postcards have been in use in this country for the largest part of a hundred years. Examination of the cards in our collection reveals that although a large proportion were used to convey messages via the post, many remain in the state as purchased. As today, these cards were bought to take home as reminders of places visited and/or to add to collections, which were much in vogue at the start of this century.

Cards were relatively cheap to post – half a penny (a fifth of today's penny) until after the first world war, and postal collections and deliveries very frequent. Postcards were used to advise those at home of safe arrival, times of departure, arrangements for visits, hotel/apartment conditions, state of the weather (not always complimentary), medical treatments received (in the case of Woodhall Spa) etc., and as advertisements for businesses and accommodation.

Woodhall Spa without doubt owes its existence and much of its beautiful woodland to a John Parkinson who was born near Horncastle in 1772. John was reputed to have had three ambitions – to create a new city (only realised in part as New Bolinbroke), plant a forest (300 acres on the moors – Roughton Wood, Kirkby Wood and Kirkby Low Wood) and to sink a coal mine.

A shaft ten feet in diameter was sunk on a moor near Woodhall in 1811. At about 500 feet, water flooded the shaft but work continued to over six hundred feet. To reach this depth, very dangerous, around-the-clock work involving the use of explosives was required. One worker died and others were injured. It is said that in order to prolong their employment, workmen took coal pieces down the shaft and produced them on their return as evidence that coal existed below. They were so convincing that at one point the bells of Horncastle were rung to celebrate their feigned success. Work was abandoned in 1823-4 and John was bankrupt. The shaft was covered over and became filled with water.

Woodhall Spa is indebted to the Lord of Woodhall Manor, Thomas Hotchkin. Finding the water helped his gout, he had the water drawn into a bath in a pump house in 1838. With an eye to future development, he financed the building of the superb Victoria Hotel in 1839. The spa was taking off as a fashionable health resort: over two thousand a year were treated in the 1840s. With the advent of the railway, numbers increased dramatically.

Steam power arrived in 1876 to raise the water and heat it. Electrolytic treatment began.

In the early 1880s, Woodhall Spa consisted of Spa Baths, the Victoria Hotel, St. Andrew's Church and fewer than ten houses.

Eagle Lodge was built in the 1870s and opened as a hotel in 1882. The bath house was up-dated in 1887 and two years later the Victoria Hotel was improved for the comfort of an ever-increasing number of visitors, including those from as far afield as India and Australasia.

Towards the end of the eighteenth century an architect from London, Richard Adolphus Came, was commissioned to plan a small garden city with a broadway lined with trees and a shopping area. Trees were planted before roads were made. He came to live in the Royal Hydro Hotel complex he had designed and later at Heatherlea.

2. Locals and visitors found the water helped a variety of complaints. Most bathed in the water, some drank it – a very salty laxative. The water had more bromine and iodine than any other, and six times as much iodine as that of the German spa Kreuznach. Woodhall Spa became 'The English Kreuznach'. This A.W.K. Morton & Son (Horncastle and Woodhall Spa) card shows the main building with a facia. It was published about 1920.

3. The Pump Room about 1920 on a photographic card by Kirkby. The bath chair awaits an occupant and heads (all hatted) turn in expectation. Donkey-drawn bath chairs were available locally from Mr. Wield.

The Alexandra Hospital was built in 1890 and the Home for Gentlewomen in 1893/4. The golf course was opened a year later. In 1897 the Royal Hydro Hotel complex opened – another major amenity for Woodhall Spa.

Woodhall Spa became an Urban District in 1898 and by the end of the century there were over a hundred houses – a quarter of which were boarding/lodging houses – and about ten shops. The population was under a thousand, double that in 1880 and rising to over sixteen hundred by 1921.

In 1905 the attractive Tea House in the Woods was opened. Petwood was also completed this year, to become an hotel in 1933.

After the first world war, Woodhall Spa Baths Trust eventually took over ownership of the Baths.

The Victoria Hotel was destroyed by fire in 1920 at the start of a decade of decline for Woodhall Spa. The population dwindled to about thirteen hundred in 1931 and the Royal Hotel was said to be virtually deserted. On a brighter note, the Pavilion Cinema (later The Kinema in the Woods) was opened in 1922 and remains an attraction to this day.

The Jubilee Gardens (a gift to the town from the Weigalls) were opened in 1935 to provide good sports facilities and a haven of leisure for residents and visitors alike.

The second world war saw the Royal Air Force using the Bath House as an ablutions centre, its officers accommodated in the Petwood Hotel and the Army billeted in The Royal. The latter group were fortunately on night manoeuvres when a land-mine destroyed this hotel.

Following two years of angry protest, the last passenger train went through Woodhall Spa in 1954. The train was to be replaced by the car and the coach.

In the 1970s, when the population had topped 2,250, around 17,000 attendances were recorded at the Baths.

The buildings over the spa well and the pumping engine chimney collapsed in September 1983.

Woodhall Spa owes much to John Parkinson, Thomas Hotchkin, the Weigalls and all the other entrepreneurs and goodly citizens who followed for providing the first-class hotels, picturesque woodland walks, attractions such as the Tea House and unique Kinema, transport, sporting and leisure facilities, camping and caravan sites, monuments, shops, cycle hire and the Cottage Museum. For recording its development and changes this century, we owe much to those local and national photographers and postcard publishers who provided such interesting images. In the captions, card publishers are always noted where known.

Shirley and Brian Prince
September 1992

For those interested in the history of Woodhall Spa, a visit to the Cottage Museum there is very rewarding.

Front cover: a multi-view postcard of Woodhall Spa published about 1910 by Jackson & Son of Grimsby in their 'Jay em Jay' series.

Back cover: (top) The Broadway is featured on a card by Carlton & Sons, posted from Woodhall Spa in September 1905.
(bottom) Martineau published this card of the Tea House in the Woods about 1960.

4. Interior of the Pump Room. Note the glasses – presumably for Spa water. Those taking baths exceeded 2,000 a year in the 1840s. Bromo-iodine mineral water and effervescing bromo-iodine salts became available. By 1850, warm and cold baths were available. High salt content created extra buoyancy which aided the bathing of those with ailing limbs and joints. Another treatment (Fango) involved the use of mud obtained as deposits in the well and standing tanks when they were cleaned out. The mud was used to treat pain locally. Valentine card, posted from Woodhall in September 1907.

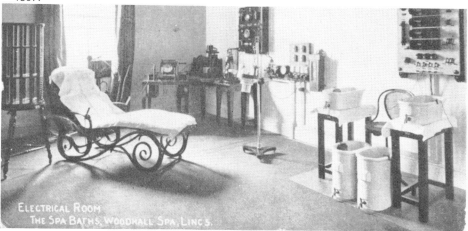

5. Electrolytic treatment began in the early 1870s, with steam power used to raise water and heat baths. A steam engine which pumped water to the surface still·works and is displayed in the Museum of Lincolnshire Life. The bath house was refurbished in 1887 to include 'shower, lave and douche', and rooms for inhalation, respiration and 'natural vapours'. Card published by Photochrom, posted at Woodhall in 1913.

SPA BATHS. WOODHALL SPA

Photo. Martineau

6. This more recent card (c.1960) by a local publisher, Martineau, shows the Spa Baths exterior has changed very little over the years. After the first world war, ownership of the baths passed eventually to the Woodhall Spa Baths Trust. Over 50 treatments were available – courses lasting 3-4 weeks and involving about 20 baths. The well bucket was said to be capable of delivering sixteen to twenty thousand gallons of water per day.

The Church Walk — Woodhall Spa

HARRISON

7. A card by Harrison of Woodhall Spa, posted in July 1911, shows Church Walk, one of the numerous pathways through local woodland, in Autumn. This was once the route to Horncastle past the Manor House, and the path was used by Victoria Hotel residents attending services at the then Parish Church of St. Andrew on the Stixwould Road.

8. Pine Tree Avenue, sometimes entitled "Invalids' Walk". Three young ladies pose for the photographer on this Valentine card of 1914.

9. Lovers Walk, near the Kinema. Another Valentine card, posted in June 1915, and written from 'Ingledew', Woodhall Spa. *"I went down here today in my bath chair ... it was so lovely and the day perfect."*

10. Kirkby Lane, a main route to Kirkby-on-Bain, features on the earliest maps of Woodhall Spa. Posted from Coningsby in 1908, this card by local publisher Harrison captures the charm of this spot, where co-author Shirley and her twin sister spent their early days.

11. The Band Stand and Enclosure. The former was originally located near the Spa Baths and Pump Room. The writer of the card, posted at Woodhall in August 1910, was waiting for the band to play on a *"hot, sunny day"*.

12. Bands were hired from April to October. According to a listener, *"A first class orchestra discourses sweet music morning, afternoon and evening."* This anonymously-published card shows musicians and conductor – photograph taken by the drummer? The notice reads 'WOODHALL SPA ORCHESTRA: AT 11, 3.30 AND 8: CONDUCTOR MR. CHAS. H. ALLEN; PROGRAMME'.

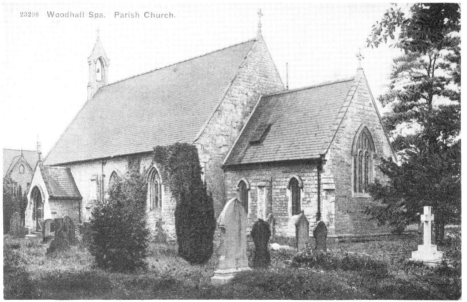

23298 Woodhall Spa. Parish Church.

13. Built mainly of stone from Stixwould Abbey, St Andrew's was the small parish church dating from 1846. It could seat 160 people in 1906. This Photochrom card, posted in 1918, gives a clear picture of a fine church.

S. ANDREW'S CHURCH AND WAR MEMORIAL, WOODHALL SPA.

14. The village school (now a garden centre) was erected nearby in 1847. The church was taken down as unsafe after the last war — it is said that the land-mine which hit the Royal Hotel diagonally opposite weakened its fabric. The churchyard remains. Local publisher Neale issued this card, posted in 1941.

St. Andrew's Church, Woodhall Spa

15. A card published by G.W. Wilson of Aberdeen, posted at Tattershall in October 1911, shows the interior of St. Andrew's with its open timber roof and elaborate carvings of angels. Note the intricate pew end carvings. Stone roof supports were carved with the arms of the Rev. E. Walker, his wife, the Dymokes and Hotchkins. E. Walker and his son (also a clergyman) are buried in the churchyard.

St. Peter's Church, Woodhall Spa

16. St Peter's Church, built in 1893 to seat 5-600 at a cost of just over £2,000. This G.W. Wilson card, posted at Horncastle in August 1908, shows foreground open space, where the chapel now stands, young trees lining The Broadway, and rustic seat on Iddesleigh Road, named after Lord Iddesleigh (Sir Stafford Northcote) a member of a group formed in 1886 to develop the spa baths.

Interior of Woodhall Spa Church.   Carlton & Sons Copyright.

17. Interior of St Peter's Church. The pulpit was given in memory of T.J. Stafford Hotchkin by his son and the brass lectern by his widow. This card by Carlton & Sons was posted at Tattershall in August 1912. Note the oak chairs, now replaced by pews, and the old lighting. A later card shows wood wall panelling, central heating, and new lighting.

18. The Catholic Church, built in 1896 to seat two hundred and dedicated to Our Lady and St Peter. This church is off Stanhope Road (named after the Stanhopes of Revesby) and was established following a mission from Grantham. Marshall, Keene & Co. of London published this card about 1912.

19. The Methodist Chapel was built on The Broadway in 1907 at a cost of £2,500, to seat over 400 people. The chapel and schoolroom replaced the Witham Road chapel. Mr. Thompson of Louth designed and built the tower and spire seen on this card, posted in 1913. Note the young trees at the roadside and the railway crossing in the right distance.

20. The Boston to Lincoln railway was built in 1848, with the Horncastle-Woodhall Junction line opened seven years later. This Photochrom 'Sepiatone' series card published c.1909 shows quite a busy station, which had a lending library and bookstall. The tall building on the right is 'Woodlands'.

Woodhall Spa from Station   Valentines Series   49215

21. A 1906 view of the line towards Kirkstead on this Valentine card shows on the left the premises now occupied by the Co-op — previously the Misses Rose toy shop and Forsters grocery. The card message includes *"we have got 3 bands playing here now."*

22. A card of 1950s vintage published by Frisby shows the Mall on the left. The line, taken over by the London and North Eastern Railway in 1923, was proposed for closure in July 1952, leading to many objections. Only an average of 21 passengers used the service daily, though, and the last passenger train left Horncastle at 7.57 p.m. on Saturday, 11th September 1954. Black crepe was tied to the door handles, and Woodhall Spa provided a wreath for the engine. The line finally closed in April 1971 and now forms part of the Viking Way.

23. W.A. Dickinson's garage and 'The Stocking Box' are featured on this W.K. Morton card, posted in August 1947.

STATION ROAD, WOODHALL SPA   PHOTO MARTINEAU

24. Bryant's shoe shop and Setchfield's hairdressing shop/cafe (premises now occupied by De Vere, and King's newsagents) feature on this card published by Martineau around 1950.

S 9602   BROADWAY, WOODHALL SPA.

25. The Broadway was a major feature of the small garden city envisaged by Richard Adolphus Came at the end of the nineteenth century. This 1912 card of an almost deserted Broadway in W.H. Smith's 'Kingsway' series features the Eagle Lodge Hotel on the right.

TATTERSALL ROAD.

26. Tattershall Road in 1906, portrayed by J. Richardson of Woodhall Spa, with the London and Manchester Stores at Chapman's corner, demolished after the second world war. Opposite, the Royal Hotel stands on what is now the Royal Square. The railway crossing is in the background; a trio of gas lamps on the traffic island were mounted on a sewer ventilation pipe.

27. A photographic card of the London and Manchester Stores published in 1905. *"I am just sending you this photo of my shop."* went the message. Chapman's shop supplied drapery, food and hardware. Advertisements for 'Lifebuoy Royal Disinfectant Soap' and 'Sunlight Soap' appear on the wall on Witham Road, while the end of Church Walk appears in the foreground.

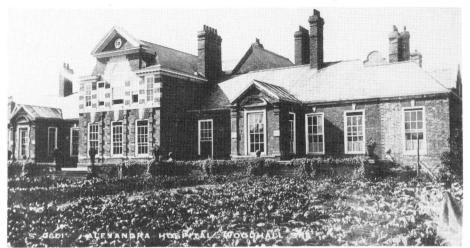

28. The Alexandra Hospital was built for £3,000 to replace a tiny hospital opened for the poor in 1873. It was named after the Danish wife of King Edward VII and opened by Countess Brownlow in 1890. Four years later, it was enlarged to accommodate 20-30 patients, and advertised in the 1930s as catering for "the treatment of rheumatism and nervous disorders". It is now the 'Alexandra'. Card by W.H. Smith in the 'Kingsway' series, posted by a patient in August 1913.

THE VICTORIA HOTEL, WOODHALL SPA
HARRISON   WOODHALL SPA.

29. The luxurious Victoria Hotel and the bath house were built in landscaped gardens by the Lord of Woodhall Manor, Thomas Hotchkin, at a cost of £30,000. The hotel stood close to the Spa Baths and Pump Room in ten acres of grounds, almost on the site of the Coronation Hall. It boasted 150 rooms with electric light and telephone in 1906. Fishing tickets for the Rivers Bain and Witham were available to residents. A Harrison of Woodhall Spa card, posted in 1907.

HARRISON

THE BROADWA

30. A cartload of trunks and boxes outside the station i feature on this card by Harrison of Woodhall Spa, pub

OODHALL SPA·

WOODHALL SPA·

what was Overton and Sons' house and apartment office
907.

Victoria Hotel from S. Woodhall Spa

75739 JV

31. The Victoria Hotel was refurbished in 1884. At one time, residents paid twelve shillings (60p) per day. A Golfer's Special Weekend including first class rail fare from King's Cross and full board was advertised for two pounds fifteen shillings (275p). Unfortunately, the Victoria was burnt down in the early hours of Easter Sunday morning, April 4th 1920, shortly after redecoration. An electrical fault in the boiler room caused a fire which spread to the linen room above. Ironically, Woodhall and Horncastle fire brigades were hampered by low mains water pressure. Lincoln's new fire engine was said to have developed a broken rear axle ten miles away. This Valentine card (75739JV) shows a summer view of the extended hotel.

32. The Royal Hydro Hotel was opened in 1897, providing 120 rooms, shops and flats with gardens, bandstand and tennis courts. A high water tower afforded fine views over the surrounding countryside. Its dance floor was said to be the biggest in Lincolnshire. By 1920, though, it was virtually deserted apart from the Mall Hotel and Winter Gardens (the most beautiful in England). It was demolished by a land-mine in August 1943. The land is now an open space — Royal Square — laid out as gardens, with a memorial to No. 617 Squadron ("The Dam Busters"), who flew Lancasters from Woodhall during the war. This c.1910 card was by the Cotswold Publishing Co.

33. Another card of the Royal Hydro Hotel, posted to Lincoln in April 1910.

34. Grace Maple (daughter of Sir John Blundell Maple of furniture fame) built her country home in her 'pet' wood near the Spa Baths in 40 acres of gardens. It became a hotel in 1933 and a year later fire burnt out the larger part of the East wing. Anonymously-published photographic card.

Petwood Hotel, Woodhall Spa

35. The house was furnished by Maples and their craftsmen are believed to have been responsible for the carving and woodwork of the staircase. This close-up view shows the entrance with its splendid woodwork.

36. In 1910 Grace Maple married Captain Archibald Weigall. They entertained on a vast scale. Famous guests included King George V, Lady Louis Mountbatten and Sir Donald Campbell. The Royal Air Force took over Petwood from 1943-5 and it became the officers' mess for the famous 'Dam-Busters' (No. 617 Squadron). Neale of Woodhall Spa provided this postcard of Atalanta's Temple with woodland backdrop. Note the intricate ironwork of the temple roof.

37. Petwood Lodge stands on the site of a blacksmith's cottage and forge. It appears here on a card posted in 1913 – now no longer the property of the hotel.

38. The Golf Hotel was at one time known as the Clevedon Club, claimed to be lit throughout by acetylene gas at the turn of the century. It was later known as the Clevedon Hotel. This card is of c.1912 vintage.

"GOLF HOTEL, WOODHALL SPA."

39. It was formerly a boys' boarding school, 'Clevedon House Preparatory School', run by the Stokoe brothers, who were involved in the laying out of the golf course. This anonymously-published card was posted in 1937 by a person receiving a variety of spa treatments. *"We saw the doctor this morning. I had a mud pack before tea and tomorrow shall have a very hot iodine bath. It is being arranged at the moment and tomorrow will enter the 'Fog'."*

Golf Club House, Woodhall Spa. *Carlton & Sons, Copyright.*

40. Golf was first played in Woodhall Spa in 1889 near Tattershall Road on a nine hole course. It was replaced in 1895 by one with the first tee near where the Kinema is. A championship course was laid down in 1903 by Harry Vardon on sandy woodland, suitable for winter golf, surrounded by birch and pine trees. Wells were sunk to provide water for the greens. A Carlton and Sons card, posted in 1905, shows teas being enjoyed outside the club house.

41. Member's subscription to the Golf Club in 1906 – Gentlemen two guineas (210p), Ladies one guinea (105p), Visitors two shillings (10p) per day, one pound per month. This Neale of Woodhall Spa card, posted in 1927, gives a clear picture of the club house.

42. Said to be possibly the finest inland golf course in Britain, Woodhall Spa golf course is considered a 'site of special interest' by the Nature Conservancy Council. Sand and heather very much in evidence on this card by Neale of Woodhall Spa. The bunkers are mini-deserts.

Eagle Hotel, Woodhall Spa

43. The Eagle Lodge Hotel, originally Eagle House when built in the mid-1870s by Charles Blyton. It became a hotel in 1882, and was refurbished seven years later. The building served more recently as a local authority old people's home. Anonymously-published card shows a rear view of this beautiful building. It was posted to Ripon in 1928 by a hotel resident.

44. The Tea House has been one of the main attractions of Woodhall Spa since it was built early this century. In its peaceful woodland setting, it has been the subject of many postcards over the years. This one, by E.W. Peakome of Boston, was posted to a Miss Hooker of Dorchester in June 1905 with the message *"Hope you will get a nice fat mail today!"* The board on the tree advises *'The Tea House: Library: Tea and Light Refreshments: Fancy Goods'.*

45. Initially run by the Misses Williams, the Tea House provided one of the first lending libraries in Woodhall Spa; gifts for sale included their own embroidery. Posted from Lincoln in 1907, this anonymously-published card shows two ladies (the Misses Williams?) and a serving girl standing at a respectable distance.

46. It has been described as *"A pretty tea-house where tea and dainty confections may be enjoyed while the ear is charmed by The Woodhall Symphony Orchestra at the band-stand nearby."* This card by Neale of Woodhall Spa shows an extended building in its splendid woodland setting. It remained virtually unchanged externally until comparatively recently.

47. Hartington House High School on The Broadway was a boarding and day school for girls, designed by Richard Adolphus Came, who planned the town itself. The principals, the Misses Lunn (Katie and Sally) insisted on French being spoken in the house.

48. Originally a tennis/cricket pavilion in the spacious grounds of Petwood, the Kinema in the Woods was converted from an Edwardian concert pavilion to the 'Pavilion Cinema' in 1922. The 68th cinema to be opened in England, it was patronised by royalty staying at Petwood. A 'phantom' orchestra accompanied silent films until the talkies arrived in 1928. An advertisement in 1937 advised:- *"This attractive Kinema is unique in many respects. It is situated amongst the pine woods, and while well furnished with comfortable plush seats, deck chairs and cushions are provided for those who appreciate them."* When the time came for the licence to be renewed in the Kinema's fiftieth year, it was granted without fee. It is to the credit of those responsible that any necessary upgrading of its facilities has not lead to any significant change in its external appearance.

"I am having the treatment, 'fog', nebulizers, vapourizers and so on. I think it is clearing my chest somewhat. This is a very quiet little place, but very pretty, with lovely grounds in which to stroll, fine woods and heather-like land. The weather unfortunately is rotten ...!" (message on a card posted from Woodhall Spa in August 1941).

Tor o Mor House, Woodhall Spa.

49. The Gentlewomen's Home was built in 1893-4 to accommodate twenty ladies needing spa treatment but who found themselves 'in reduced circumstances'. This anonymously-published card refers to this Home as Tor o Mor House and was posted to Leeds in 1937.

COPYRIGHT W.S.3.   THE GENTLEWOMAN'S HOME. S. WOODHALL SPA.   LILYWHITE LTD., THE PHOTO PRINTERS.

50. Four bungalows combined, the Home was extended in 1915 and used as a Red Cross hospital in the first world war. It is now the Fairlawns Nursing Home. This view shows the Home, now devoid of ivy, on a Lilywhite card posted in 1937.

Frisby. Royal Jubilee Park Swimming Pool, Woodhall Spa.

51. The Jubilee Gardens were originally laid out by the Weigalls for their lavish garden parties. A Frisby card posted to Hull in July 1935 illustrates the swimming pool and contemporary swimwear.

JUBILEE CAFE & PADDLING POOL, WOODHALL SPA   Photo: Martineau

52. The gardens in the Royal Jubilee Park were given to the town to celebrate King George V's Silver Jubilee and opened by HRH Princess Marie Louise in 1935. Much activity around the cafe on this 1950s card by Martineau.

SWIMMING POOL, JUBILEE GARDENS, WOODHALL SPA · PHOTO MARTINEAU

53. The Park includes a heated open-air swimming pool and facilities for bowling, tennis etc. Another Martineau card, posted from the Eagle Lodge Hotel in 1946, gives a closer view of the pool.

THE LAWSON HOTEL, WOODHALL SPA

54. The Lawson Hotel, known as the Spa Hotel, was earlier the Northcote Hydro (run by Doctor Cuffe) and the Hotel Goring. It was situated on the corner opposite St Peter's Church, where new buildings now stand. Card by Harrison of The Vale, Woodhall Spa.

55. Raftsund, formerly a guest house, is now the girls' boarding house for St. Hugh's School. Anonymously-published card posted to Sussex in September 1907.

56. Woodlands was the home of Dr. Gwyn at the corner of Stanhope Avenue and The Broadway. It later became a hotel. Once also a primary school, it was converted to retail premises. This card by J. Wield of Woodhall was sent to Portsmouth in September 1915 by a guest.

57. A card by Harrison featuring Humpherson & Co.'s shop (General builders, furnishing ironmongers, cycles, all kinds of golf and tennis requisites) on Tattershall Road. It was addressed to Eadie in Redditch (for whom the shop was an agent), requesting a cycle nut. A variety of wheeled vehicles can be seen in front, from pushchair to motor cycle (CE 9). 'Beaufort high-grade cycles' were made in the nearby works.

VICTORIA LODGE, WOODHALL SPA.

58. Victoria Lodge, adjacent to Hartington House, served as an annex to the Lunn's school for young ladies. A pre-first world war view of this fine building.